Teacher's Book

MORE! 3

Gerngross · Puchta · Holzmann
Kamauf · Williams

Teil B: Worksheets

Enriched course

HELBLING

MORE! 3 ENRICHED COURSE TEACHER'S BOOK – TEIL B

by
Günter Gerngross
Herbert Puchta
Christian Holzmann
Ulrike Kamauf
Gerry Williams

www.helbling.com

Edited by Johanna Schmölzer, Valerie Meller, Verena Rainer
Design and layout by Heinz Hanuschka
Illustrated by Svjetlan Junaković, Roberto Battestini, Francesca Carabelli, Matteo Settegrana, Giovanni Giorgi Pierfranceschi, Lorenzo Sabbatini

Printed by Athesia

First published 2018, second print run 2019

ISBN 978-3-99045-754-2

Inhalt

Worksheet	Komplexitätsgrad	Einsatz	Seite
Unit 1			
Worksheet 1	□■□	9	4
Worksheet 2	■□□	5	5
Worksheet 3	□■□	Grammar	6
Worksheet 4	□■□	11	7
Unit 2			
Worksheet 1	□■□	3	8
Worksheet 2	■□□	5	9
Worksheet 3	□□■	10	10
Worksheet 4	□■□	Grammar	11
Unit 3			
Worksheet 1	□■□	Grammar	12
Worksheet 2	□□■	5	13
Worksheet 3	□□■	7	14
Worksheet 4	□■□	12	15
Unit 4			
Worksheet 1	□■□	4	16
Worksheet 2	□■□	9	17
Worksheet 3	■□□	Grammar	18
Worksheet 4	□■□	Grammar	19
Unit 5			
Worksheet 1	□■□	3	20
Worksheet 2	□■□	11	21
Worksheet 3	■□□	Grammar	22
Worksheet 4	□□■	14	23
Unit 6			
Worksheet 1	□■□	6	24
Worksheet 2	□□■	9	25
Worksheet 3	■□□	Grammar	26
Worksheet 4	□□■	Grammar	27
Unit 7			
Worksheet 1	□■□	Grammar	28
Worksheet 2	□■□	8	29
Worksheet 3	□■□	12	30
Worksheet 4	□□■	14	31
Unit 8			
Worksheet 1	□■□	Grammar	32
Worksheet 2	□■□	3	33
Worksheet 3	□■□	17	34
Worksheet 4	□□■	21	35
Unit 9			
Worksheet 1	□■□	4	36
Worksheet 2	■□□	8	37
Worksheet 3	□■□	10	38
Worksheet 4	□□■	10	39
Unit 10			
Worksheet 1	□□■	Grammar	40
Worksheet 2	□□■	6	41
Worksheet 3	□■□	13	42
Worksheet 4	■□□	Grammar	43
Unit 11			
Worksheet 1	□■□	3	44
Worksheet 2	□■□	6	45
Worksheet 3	□□■	7	46
Worksheet 4	□■□	Grammar	47
Unit 12			
Worksheet 1	■□□	Grammar	48
Worksheet 2	□■□	5	49
Worksheet 3	□■□	Grammar	50
Worksheet 4	□□■	15	51
Unit 13			
Worksheet 1	□■□	Grammar	52
Worksheet 2	□□■	8	53
Worksheet 3	□■□	11	54
Worksheet 4	□□■	13	55
Extra Unit 14			
Worksheet 1	□■□	9	56
Worksheet 2	□□■	6	57
Worksheet 3	□■□	Grammar	58
Worksheet 4	□□■	11	59

Vereinfachte Lesetexte

Playing for others (U1)	60
James Holman: the record traveller (U3)	61
Mary Kingsley: a Victorian lady in Africa (U3)	62
Candyman (U6)	63
Alessia (U7)	65
Nikola Tesla: The man who invented the 20th century (U8)	66
Castaway! (U12)	67

■□□ Aufgabenstellung niedriger Komplexität, □■□ Aufgabenstellung mittlerer Komplexität, □□■ Aufgabenstellung höherer Komplexität

1 **Claire interviews her grandmother Martha for her school magazine about *The Beatles*. Complete the questions and put them into the dialogue.**

What / your favourite *Beatles* album?
Who / be / your favourite band member?
Who / your favourite band?
You / ever / see / *The Beatles* play live?
What / you / think of them now, about fifty years after they broke up?
When / you / listen / to a *Beatles* song for the first time?

Claire 1 ....

Martha My favourite band? Definitely *The Beatles*.

Claire 2 ....

Martha When my older brother played their first single "Love Me Do". I was 15 then, and I loved their music.

Claire 3 ....

Martha I saw them live on my 17th birthday when they played their first US concert in Washington DC. It was amazing, with thousands of screaming fans. And I was one of them!

Claire 4 ....

Martha Well ... let me think ... *Sergeant Pepper's Lonely Hearts Club Band.* I really think that was their best album ever.

Claire 5 ....

Martha John Lennon. I was really shocked when I heard about his death.

Claire 6 ....

Martha I still think that they are one of the best bands in the world. I still listen to their music and old records. I've got all of them!

Claire Thank you for the interesting interview!

nach SB p. 12

1 **Write in the words from the box. Use the present simple.**

find
know
be
take
not look
make
have got
give
be
waste
be

At an audition

"Kim, you [1]........................ a fantastic singer. You [2]........................ what it [3]........................ to be a superstar! Great voice, great looks and you [4]........................ how to dance too. I'm sure your mother [5]........................ very proud of you: she told us that you didn't want to come! Well, we're glad you did! It was definitely the thing to do – we will see you again next week!"

"Kevin, I'm afraid* there is nothing we can do for you, you [1]........................ out of the competition. Don't [2]........................ your time – [3]........................ a real job and [4]........................ up singing. You [5]........................ like a pop star and you're never going to [6]........................ it."

VOCABULARY
***I'm afraid ...** – Ich befürchte ... / Leider ...

nach SB p. 11

1 Put the verbs into the past simple to complete the story.

The Heavy Drums

Neil [1].. (dream) of becoming a superstar one day. His older brother Mike [2].. (be) in a band, *The Heavy Drums*, and they [3].. (practise) every Sunday afternoon in the basement* of their house. Mike [4].. (play) the drums and Neil always [5].. (watch) them play. One day Neil [6].. (feel) really bored, so he [7].. (go) down to the basement.

He [8].. (take) his older brother's drumsticks* and slowly [9].. (start) to play. This [10].. (go) on for quite a while. When he [11].. (be) alone at home, he always[12].. (practise). Nobody [13].. (know) that Neil [14].. (be) quite good at playing the drums. He [15].. (love) his secret new hobby and the hours that he [16].. (spend) in the basement.

One day, Mike [17].. (fall) off his bike coming home from school and [18].. (break) his arm. It [19].. (be) a week before the band's performance in the school's talent show. His arm [20].. (be) in plaster*, so he [21].. (can not) play. *The Heavy Drums* [22].. (meet) to talk about the situation. They [23].. (have) no idea how to perform without their drummer. It was a big surprise when Neil [24].. (tell) them that he [25].. (can) play the drums. He [26].. (sit) down at the drums and [27].. (get) started. The band [28].. (can not) believe it, he [29].. (be) great! So *The Heavy Drums* [30].. (play) at the show – and they [31].. (win)! Then Neil [32].. (know) what he [33].. (have to) do: He [34].. (want) to start his own band and become the next superstar.

VOCABULARY: *basement – Keller; **drumsticks** – Trommelstöcke; **plaster** – Gips

nach SB p. 13

1 **Write a text (100–120 words) about your favourite song. These questions might help you:**

My favourite song

What is the song about?
What do you like best about it? Is it the lyrics / the tune / the rhythm?
Which musical style is it?
Who sings it? Describe her/him.
What does she/he want to say with this song?

....

....

....

....

....

....

....

....

....

....

....

....

....

....

....

....

....

....

....

....

....

....

....

....

nach SB p. 13

1 Complete the text with the sentences from the box.

What a coincidence!

Let's see what our next caller has to say.
We had the same family name – Gorman – which is strange, isn't it?
Our guest today is Sam, who would like to tell us about strange coincidences in his life.
We decided that we should really meet and talk about these strange coincidences.
We first met in a chat room and I really liked talking to her. She seemed really nice.

Host* Hi, and welcome again to *Live on Air*.

1 ....

Hi, Sam. Tell us more!

Guest Hi, my name's Sam and I'm from Birmingham. Today I'd like to tell you about how I met my girlfriend, Cathy. 2 ....

....

We quickly found out that we had the same hobbies – she also loves roller-skating, going to the cinema, and travelling. But the really strange thing happened when she gave me her name and address: 3 ....

....

Well, some days later she gave me her phone number and guess what – Cathy's number started with 2167, exactly like mine! 4 ....

....

Then Cathy told me that she would be away on a holiday – she was going to Rome for a week. I was really surprised to hear it – I was going to Rome, too! We met up at the airport and sat next to each other on the plane. And that's how we became friends.

Host Incredible! What a story! It's hard to believe, isn't it?

5 ....

....

VOCABULARY
***host** – Gastgeber/in

nach SB p. 16

1 **What were the people doing when the accident happened? Write sentences using the past continuous.**

....

....

....

....

....

....

....

....

....

....

....

....

....

....

....

....

nach SB p. 17

1 **Read the story and tick T (*True*) or F (*False*).**

Lightning strikes*

John McAlister grew up in a small village in Scotland. As a boy he loved going for long walks in the hills with his friends. One day a terrible thunderstorm started when the boys were up in the hills. There was nothing to protect them, so they lay down on the ground. Suddenly lightning flashed with a loud roar of thunder* and struck young John! Luckily he wasn't hurt badly and his friends helped him get down the hill safely. He couldn't move his right leg for a week, but he soon got well again. After that, John didn't go for walks in the hills any more. He dreamt of the south, of going to Spain and sitting in the sun. For his 18th birthday his family surprised him with a ticket to Spain. He would spend two weeks there, in a wonderful hotel. John was happy.

A month later he was on his way to Spain. He spent his time lying in the sun on the beach and watching the other people. One day he had an idea. He wanted to go on a boat trip. John hadn't sailed a boat very often before, but he thought it was the perfect day for a trip. There wasn't a cloud in the sky. The sea was calm, so he hired a boat and set sail*. After a wonderful boat trip along the coast, John wanted to go back. But suddenly he heard and saw it: the sky had turned black and there was a thunderstorm! John tried to stay calm, but his heart was beating fast. Would he reach the harbour safely? With a loud crash lightning struck his boat and it broke into three pieces. Luckily for John the coast guard arrived very quickly and saved him. It was amazing. The local newspapers interviewed him and wrote stories about the strange coincidence.

VOCABULARY
***lightning** – Blitz; **strike** – treffen, einschlagen; **with a loud roar of thunder** – mit einem lauten Donnergroll; **set sail** – in See stechen

		T	F
1	John McAlister grew up in a town in Scotland.	☐	☐
2	One day he was playing in the garden when a thunderstorm came.	☐	☐
3	Lightning struck him, but he wasn't hurt badly.	☐	☐
4	He walked down the hill without help.	☐	☐
5	For his 18th birthday his family gave him a ticket to Spain.	☐	☐
6	He spent his days lying on the beach and learning how to sail.	☐	☐
7	On his boat trip the sky suddenly turned black.	☐	☐
8	The boat broke into pieces, but John McAlister didn't die.	☐	☐

nach SB p. 20

1 Past simple or past continuous? Complete the sentences.

A A thief [1].. (see) that a woman [2]... (talk) on her mobile. He [3].. (decide) that he [4].. (want) to steal the woman's handbag.

B A woman [1].. (walk) down a street when suddenly she [2].. (hear) a cry. She [3].. (look) up and [4]... (see) a baby that [5].. (fall) towards her. She [6].. (catch) it.

C Some boys [1]... (play) football when one of them [2]...................................... (break) his arm. Some girls [3]... (watch) the match. They [4].. (call) an ambulance for him.

1 **Complete the sentences with *before, after, while, during, until, when* or *by the time.***

The Maths lesson

Yesterday we had a Maths lesson with our teacher Ms Lennox. [1].. it started, I wanted to talk to my friend Sue, but she didn't arrive [2].. a few seconds before Ms Lennox came into the classroom. [3].. the lesson I was really bored. I didn't listen to Ms Lennox. [4].. she was writing on the board, I was writing a note to Sue. [5].. I finished my letter, I tried to pass it on* to her. [6].. Ms Lennox was explaining something, I folded* the note.

[7].. Ms Lennox suddenly looked at me, she saw that I wasn't working. "I'd like to talk to you after the lesson, Christopher," she said to me. [8].. the rest of the lesson I had to sit at the front.

[9].. the bell finally rang, Ms Lennox told me that I had some work to do. [10].. the break I had to copy the missing exercises from the board. No break! I couldn't talk to Sue and I couldn't invite her to come to the cinema with me tonight, and [11].. the break was over, Sue was in another lesson. [12].. I saw her later outside, she said, "Serves you right," and walked past me. Life's not fair!

VOCABULARY
***pass sth on** – etwas weitergeben; **fold** – zusammenfalten

nach SB p. 31

1 **On her journeys to West Africa, Mary Kingsley kept a diary. Look at the notes below. Then write about what happened during her trips (120–180 words).**

1893 first trip: Angola, Congo, Cameroon, Nigeria
live with people, eat their food - collect rare fish - a few adventures - leopard, hippos, crocodile

1895 second trip: steamboat Ogooué River
visit Fang people - on foot - cannibals - bag with human body parts - finish trip: climb Mount Cameroon - men too weak

Here is the beginning:

April, 1893

My first trip to Africa. It was always my dream to come here and live with the people of Angola, Congo, Cameroon and Nigeria in their huts and eat their food. ...

1 Fill in the missing verbs in the present or past tense to complete Christine's letter from Florida.

record
hire
go
spend
drive
be (4x)
have to
can
have got
take
arrive
explain
like
get

Dear Caroline,

We're having a fantastic time in Florida. Mum and I [1].. last week and [2].. six days in Disney World. It [3].. really cool. What I [4].. best was of course the Superstars Studios where I [5].. my own song. Now I [6].. my own CD — I will play it to you when we [7].. back.

Right now we [8].. in Wakulla Springs State Park. Mum [9].. a car and we [10].. north from Disney World. Yesterday we [11].. on a boat trip in a glass-bottom* boat. It [12].. really awesome. From our boat we [13].. see lots of large fish and even alligators! Our guide [14].. everything to us and I [15].. lots of great photos, I [16].. really close to some of the biggest alligators. I [17].. go now, Mum is going to take me to a shopping centre in Tallahassee.

See you soon.

Love,

Christine

VOCABULARY
***glass-bottom** – Glasboden

nach SB p. 27

1 **Look at the pictures and write about Mr Horton's journey, using the *take time to* structure.**

Mr Horton's long journey to Athens

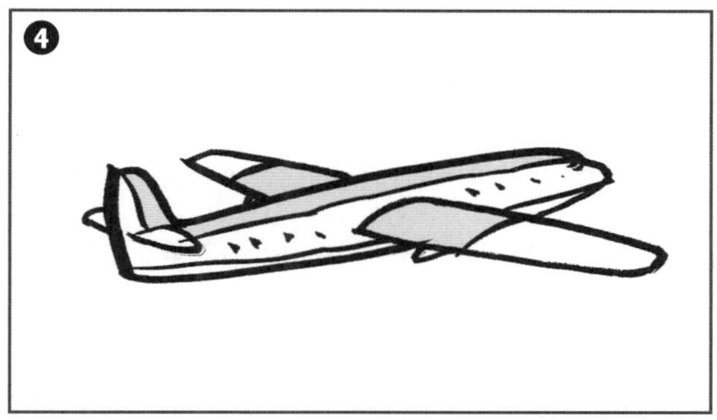

1 **Complete the text. Use the correct form of the adjectives in brackets.**

Here's what Chris, a fourteen-year-old film fan, says about animal movies:

"I must say that I really love animal movies, nature films* and cartoons. One of [1].. (old) animal films I know is *King Kong*. It was made in 1933. When people first saw it in cinemas, they were really scared, but I think today it isn't [2].. (scary) as most modern movies. It's almost [3].. (funny) to watch.

I think [4].. (scary) movie ever made is *Jaws*. I watched it with my older brother. It's [5].. (exciting) than any film I've ever seen and it has also got one of [6].. (good) soundtracks* I've heard. The music is really [7].. (awesome).

I also love animal cartoons. *Shrek* is a [8].. (good) example. It has got [9].. (cute) characters – I'm very fond of the Donkey, he's in [10].. (funny) scenes in the film. My eight-year-old sister Marie is a huge fan of the movie *The Lion King*. I don't think it's [11].. (good) as *Shrek*. My favourite cartoon is *The Emperor's New Groove*. In this film an emperor turns into a llama* and has to get back to the throne*. The llama in the movie is [12].. (interesting) and [13].. (clever) animal of all."

VOCABULARY
***nature film** – Naturfilm; **soundtrack** – Filmmusik; **an emperor turns into a llama** – ein Kaiser verwandelt sich in ein Lama; **throne** – Thron

  nach SB p. 35

1 **Look at the pictures and write the story (120–180 words). Give names to the people in the pictures and think of an ending. Use the correct past tenses. Write sentences with *before / after / while*.**

Shark attack!

....

....

....

....

....

....

....

....

....

....

....

....

....

....

....

....

....

....

....

....

....

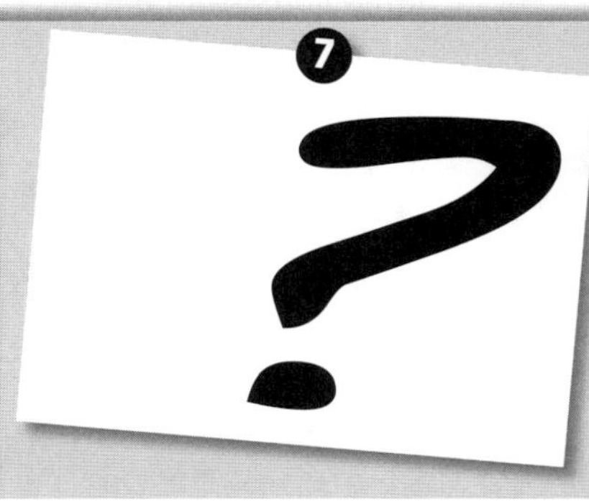

1 **Complete the sentences with the superlative form of the adjectives in brackets.**

The Appalachian Trail*

The Appalachian Trail runs for about 3,500 km and is one of [1] .... (long) trails in the world. It passes through 14 states in the east of the United States. Most of the trail is completely wild and lots of wild animals live there.

On the trail, watch out for mountain lions. They can run as fast as 55 kph and are among [2] .... (fast) animals in the world.

Black bears are also very dangerous. But they are [3] .... (aggressive) when they have to look after their young and try to defend themselves. They are among [4] .... (strong) and [5] .... (dangerous) bears and can kill humans easily. The [6] .... (bad) thing you can do is to run away. You should always move away slowly. Don't try to climb a tree – bears are good climbers!

Always watch where you put your feet – there are lots of dangerous snakes in the Appalachian Mountains. The rattlesnake* is one of [7] .... (poisonous) snakes in the mountains. There is one more animal, however, that is also very dangerous. The moose* perhaps looks like [8] .... (slow) animal of all. But it can run very fast, and can be more dangerous than a bear.

VOCABULARY
***The Appalachian Trail** – Wanderweg in den Appalachen (nordamerikan. Gebirge); **rattlesnake** – Klapperschlange; **moose** – Elch

1 **Look at the three pictures. Write sentences to compare the three places. Use the adjectives in the box.**

The perfect holiday

interesting
exciting
difficult
relaxing
expensive
dangerous
hot/cold

Example: I think skiing in the Alps is more exciting than climbing in Scotland.

....

....

....

....

....

....

....

....

....

....

....

....

nach SB p. 40

1 Match the sentence halves.

1 The Tower of London is a museum
2 The old Globe Theatre disappeared. Now there's a new Globe Theatre
3 The architect
4 Many visitors
5 Hyde Park is a great place for people
6 A scary place

☐ which looks almost the same as the old one.
☐ who love taking long walks in the fresh air.
☐ which about 2.5 million people visit every year.
☐ which is very popular is the London Dungeon – it's an underground museum of horrors.
☐ who rebuilt the City of London after the Great Fire was Christopher Wren.
☐ who come to London love shopping in Covent Garden.

2 Complete.

advance
idea
river
queues
far
view
ride
book
giant

The London Eye is a [1]................ wheel on the South Bank of the [2]................ not [3]................ from the Houses of Parliament. The 25-minute [4]................ gives you a great [5]................ of London. You can [6]................ your ride in [7]................ . This is usually a good [8]................ because there are often long [9]................ .

1 **Steve, a 14-year-old boy from London, recommends some places for visitors. Complete the text with the places in the box.**

Welcome to London!

Madame Tussauds
the River Thames
Tate Modern
the Tower of London
the London Dungeon
the London Eye
Tower Bridge
Oxford Street

London is a fantastic city. I like living here very much and if you ever get a chance to visit London, you must go to some of the following places. When you first come to the city, take a boat trip on [1].. . From there you can see some very interesting places: [2].. , for example. It's a beautiful old castle and you can see some of the Queen's jewels there. If you're lucky, you'll see a big ship going down the Thames and they will raise [3].. so that the ship can pass through. If it's a sunny day, get off at [4].. and go on the ride. From the top there are some great views of London. After seeing the sights you should go to [5].. . It's one of the longest shopping streets in the world. The music shops are brilliant there. But before you go shopping, maybe you should take a short walk from the London Eye to [6].. . It's now a very popular art gallery with a great collection of modern works of art that attracts millions of visitors. And then, of course, you just have to go to one of the most popular tourist attractions of all: [7].. , the world-famous waxworks museum, and see all those famous people from history, sport or the world of entertainment. If you like a bit of a thrill, you should definitely go to [8].. . It's really creepy*. These are my favourite places in London – but come and see for yourself what you like best about the city!

VOCABULARY
***creepy** – gruselig

nach SB p. 47

1 Complete the sentences with *who* or *which*.

1 The shark .... is most feared is the great white shark.

2 Bethany is a girl .... wanted to become a professional surfer.

3 A reporter spoke to the girl .... was attacked by a shark.

4 The shark .... bit through her surfboard and her arm was three metres long.

5 Some friends .... were with her helped her get out of the water and saved her life.

6 They were waiting for the ambulance .... took her to hospital.

7 *Save Our Seas*, ... is an organisation to protect the oceans, offered her the chance to train as a photographer.

8 Bethany told her thrilling story to the reporter .... interviewed her in hospital.

1 **Fiona is on a school trip to London with her friends and her English teacher. Unfortunately, things aren't going very well for her. Read the beginning of her email. Then continue it (120–180 words). Use the ideas from the box to write the email.**

Fiona's trip to London

The next day: warmer, but heavy rain
Long queues at the museums
Cinema tickets: too expensive
Pickpockets* stole her money in Covent Garden
Fiona doesn't like English food (hamburgers, fish and chips, pizza served with rice)
She was nearly run over by a car* because English people drive on the 'wrong' side
She lost the key to her hotel room
Had an argument* with her best friend

Dear Ayla,
London is a nightmare! Since we arrived here last Saturday, everything has gone wrong. But let's start at the beginning. We had to wait for two hours because our flight was delayed. When we finally arrived in London, it was snowing, which doesn't happen very often here. It was really hard to get a taxi to the city centre.

....
....
....
....
....
....
....
....
....
....
....
....
....
....
....
....
....

VOCABULARY
***pickpocket** – Taschendieb/in; **She was nearly run over by a car.** – Sie wurde fast von einem Auto niedergefahren.; **argument** – Streit

nach SB p. 48

1 Read the following text about the American tradition of Groundhog* Day. Then tick the sentences T (*True*) or F (*False*).

Phil is a groundhog and he lives in Punxsutawney, Pennsylvania, in the USA. Every year, on February 2nd, the town holds the groundhog festival on Gobbler's Knob, a hill in Punxsutawney. There's music, there's food and a lot of people come to join the party. Then members of the Groundhog Club wake Phil from his winter sleep. He comes slowly out of his hole. The legend says* that if Phil sees his shadow* on the ground and goes back to his hole, there will be six more weeks of winter. If Phil doesn't see his shadow, it will be an early spring. Before he goes back to sleep, two men of the club also pick him up and hold him close to their ears. People believe that Phil whispers something into the men's ears. Phil speaks to the Groundhog Club president in "Groundhogese" (the language of groundhogs). Then the president translates* Phil's words into English. This day is known as Groundhog Day in the USA and in Canada. Many TV stations send their reporters to Punxsutawney and there are even live reports on TV. For more than a hundred years Phil has predicted* the weather on February 2nd. And this year he said that there would be six more weeks of winter.

VOCABULARY
***groundhog** – Murmeltier;
the legend says – die Legende besagt;
shadow – Schatten;
translate – übersetzen;
predict – vorhersagen

		T	F
1	Every year many people celebrate Phil's birthday on February 2nd.	☐	☐
2	Only the members of the Groundhog Club are allowed to come to the party.	☐	☐
3	Groundhogs usually sleep in winter.	☐	☐
4	If Phil sees his shadow on the ground, spring will come soon.	☐	☐
5	The members of the Groundhog Club also talk to him.	☐	☐
6	The groundhog can speak two languages.	☐	☐
7	There are many people who are interested in the festival and watch it on TV.	☐	☐
8	This year Phil said that spring wouldn't come soon.	☐	☐

nach SB p. 53

1 **Continue the story. What went wrong? What happened on this Friday 13th? Why did Frederick have bad luck? Write a text of 120–180 words about his day.**

Friday 13th

When Frederick got up in the morning and had a look at his calendar, he knew it wouldn't be an easy day. He was a very superstitious boy, so he was really scared when he saw a black cat crossing the street in front of him on his way to the bus stop. ...

1 **Circle the correct forms.**

Lillian's lucky day

"I think today is going to be my lucky day. I've bought a lottery ticket! If I [1] *win / will win*, I [2] *will travel / travel* to London. I [3] *take / will take* my parents and my best friend Lucy with me. If the weather [4] *is / will be* fine, we [5] *will walk / walk* around in the city and go to lots of fantastic places. If we [6] *will go / go* to London in spring or summer, we [7] *will have / have* a picnic in Hyde Park. If it [8] *will rain / rains*, we [9] *won't stay / don't stay* at the hotel. We [10] *go / will go* to one of the city's fantastic museums and art galleries. I [11] *buy / will buy* some presents – T-shirts, CDs, posters – for my friends if I [12] *have got / will have got* any money at the end of the trip. If I [13] *go / will go* and tell Lucy about my plans now, she [14] *will get / gets* excited about it all, too!"

nach SB p. 55

1 **Have a look at the Tarot cards on the table. Write sentences about them. Then design your own card (card 7) and say what it means.**

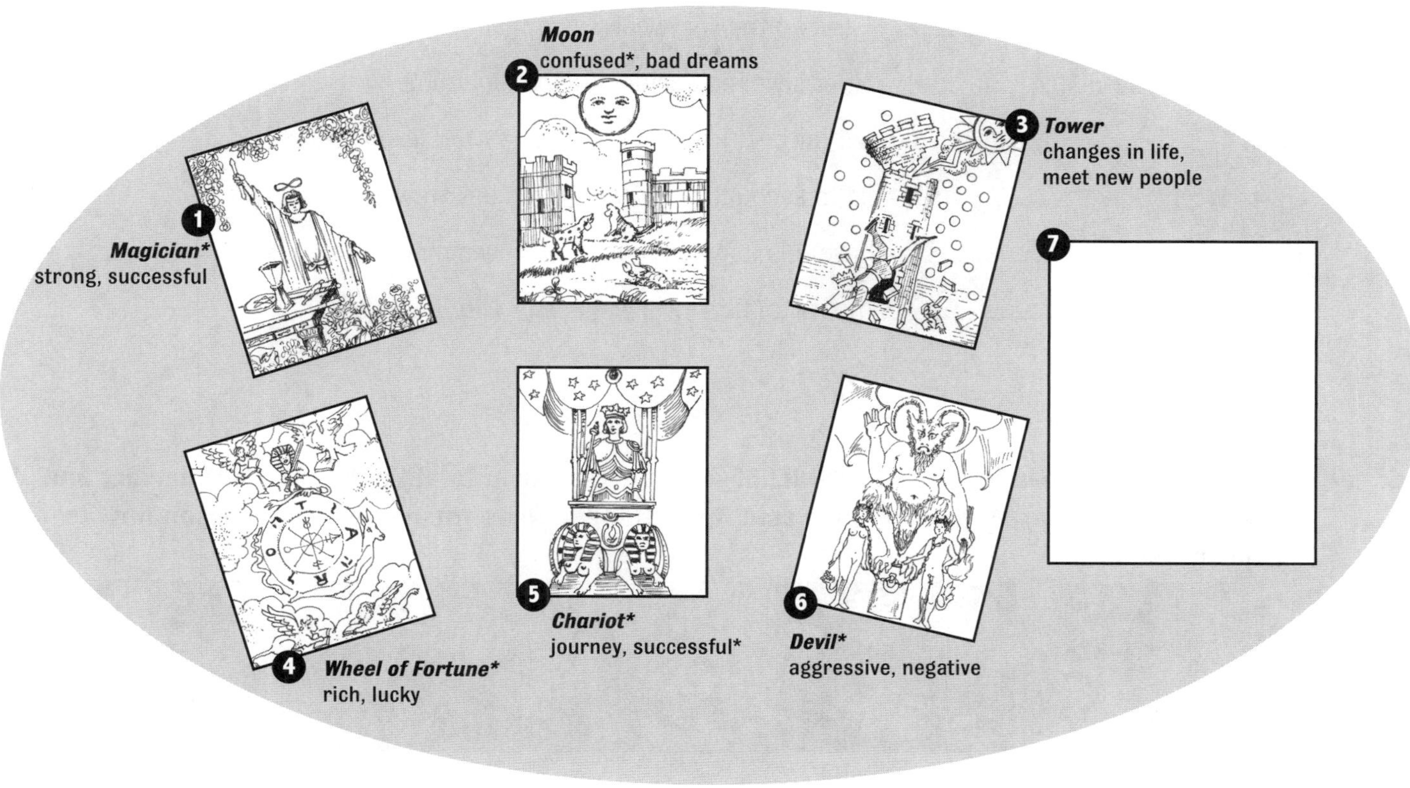

VOCABULARY
***magician** – Zauberer; **confused** – verwirrt; **successful** – erfolgreich; **wheel of fortune** – Glücksrad; **chariot** – Wagen; **devil** – Teufel

Example: If you pick the Tower, there will be many changes in your life and you will meet new people. ...

....

....

....

....

....

....

....

....

....

....

....

nach SB p. 55

1 Complete the sentences with the present perfect and circle *for* or *since*.

1 I .... (live) in this city *since* / *for* twelve years.

2 My dad .... (drive) the same car *since* / *for* six years and he .... (not have) an accident *since* / *for* 2002.

3 I .... (know) my best friend Ahmed *since* / *for* seven years.

4 We .... (sit) next to each other *since* / *for* the day we started school.

5 He .... (have) his dog Bolt *since* / *for* seven months now.

6 We .... (not take) him for a walk *since* / *for* last week.

2 Can you remember the texts in MORE! 3? Read the statements, fill in the present perfect and circle *for* or *since*. Who could have said these things? Write the name of the person next to the statement.

1 "I .... (not be) back to the beach *since* / *for* three weeks. I'm still afraid of the sea."

Name: ....

2 "I .... (be) in France *since* / *for* a month now. I really love Paris, it's a fantastic city."

Name: ....

3 "I was blind. But I .... (learn) to see *since* / *for* I started to explore the streets of London with my metal walking stick."

Name: ....

4 "I .... (not have) a strange dream like that *since* / *for* a long time. It was about eating porridge for breakfast."

Name: ....

5 "I .... (not speak) to Alessia *since* / *for* last Friday because she went away with her parents for the weekend."

Name: ....

nach SB p. 63

1 **Complete the text with the phrases from the box.**

- We've always got on so well with each other
- mind my own business
- I've fallen out with her
- she will try to make up with me
- stormed out
- couldn't think of a reason
- We've always shared

Joanne's birthday

Ashley and I have been best friends for a long time. [1].. our problems and we've told each other everything. But [2].. recently*. It happened last Saturday. It was my 13th birthday and I had a party with my friends from school and my basketball team. We had a huge buffet and even a karaoke stage, which my brother had put up in our garden. The party was fun, except for one thing: Ashley didn't come to my party! And she didn't even call me on that day. I was really disappointed and [3].. why she hadn't come. I've never forgotten HER birthday.

On Monday we met in the school cafeteria. We sat down to have lunch together. When I asked Ashley about Saturday and the party, there was a surprised look on her face. Then she told me to [4].. and [5].. of the cafeteria. We haven't talked since Monday. I have no idea what her problem is. [6].. but I certainly won't talk to her now. I don't know if [7].. .

What's the matter with her?

VOCABULARY
***recently** – vor kurzem

1 **Read the text from Pamela's diary. Then match the correct answers to the questions. There are two extra answers that you don't need.**

Relationships can be difficult sometimes. Take Alan and Monica, for example. They have been together for over a year now, but I don't think they understand what being honest really means. Normally she gets on well with him and he gets on well with her, but sometimes they fall out with each other, especially when they try to tell each other the truth. He tells her that he doesn't like her new dress, she tells him she doesn't like his favourite music ... but they soon make up and everything is fine again. Until last week. Monica wanted them both to go to a party with some of her friends. Alan said no. The truth was he didn't like her friends and he wanted to watch a football match on TV. Monica stormed out of the room and since then they are not speaking to each other. Monica is my friend, too. I asked her if she was going to break up with Alan. "Pamela," she said. "Mind your own business." "Great," I thought. "That's probably a good sign." But we'll have to wait and see. Maybe they can learn to be honest with each other after all. Best friends can do that, can't they? I can't really help them with that!

1 How long have Alan and Monica been together?
2 What is Alan and Monica's problem?
3 What usually happens when they don't agree?
4 Why did Alan and Monica fall out last week?
5 Why didn't Alan want to go to the party?
6 What did Monica do?
7 What did Monica tell Pamela?
8 What can best friends do?

- ☐ Alan didn't want to go to a party with Monica.
- ☐ She left the room angrily.
- ☐ They both wanted to go to the party.
- ☐ She told her not to interfere.
- ☐ For over a year.
- ☐ They can learn to be honest with each other.
- ☐ Monica said she didn't like football.
- ☐ He preferred football to Monica's friends.
- ☐ They make up with each other afterwards.
- ☐ They can't really be honest with each other.

nach SB p. 62

1 **Write one of the following texts (100–120 words):**

a My favourite thing

Describe something that is really important to you. Write about:

- who gave it to you / when you bought it
- what it looks like
- what is so special about it
- how often and when you use it

....

....

....

....

....

....

....

....

b My best friend

Write a text about:

- the funniest day or
- the most exciting adventure or
- the scariest moment

you've had with your best friend.

....

....

....

....

....

....

....

....

nach SB p. 63

1 Circle the correct form.

1 Tesla *invented / has invented* the first speedometer for cars.

2 In the 1880s, Nikola Tesla *developed / has developed* AC electrical current.

3 Nikola Tesla *was / has been* a very poor man when he died.

4 Today, people *realised / have realised* at last what a brilliant inventor Nikola Tesla was.

5 The ice-lolly *was / has been* an accidental invention.

6 Sadie McCallum *suffered / has suffered* from her illness for over eight years now.

7 Sadie *had / has had* complicated operations on her hips when she was seven.

8 Sadie's invention *won / has won* several more prizes since the school invention.

2 Fill in the past simple or the present perfect of the verbs in brackets.

1

Sarah .... (you / ever / hear) of an inventor called Nikola Tesla?

Patrick Yes, I have. He .... (develop) AC electrical current before Thomas Edison.

2

Carol Where's Richard? He .... (not be) to school for three days.

David I .... (call) him yesterday. He .... (have) an accident with his bike at the weekend and .... (hurt) his ankle, so he can't walk at the moment.

3

Oliver .... (you / ever / be) to the USA?

Nicole No, but I'd love to go soon.

Oliver My best friend and his family .... (just / move) there. I'm going to visit them in summer.

4

Mum .... (you / write) your report yet, Alyssa?

Alyssa Yes, Mum. I .... (do) it yesterday in the afternoon.

5

Suzanne .... (you / enjoy) the play last night?

Mike It was OK, but a bit long. I .... (leave) a bit earlier because I had to study for the test.

1 **Read the following text about a famous inventor. Then tick T (*True*) or F (*False*).**

The World Wide Web

Tim Berners-Lee is a British computer scientist who invented the World Wide Web (WWW). He was born on 8th June 1955 in London, England. After school he went to Oxford University where he studied physics. Then, in 1980, he got a job at the CERN Organisation in Switzerland where he needed to share information with different people in different places. To make this easier he discovered a way of using hypertext, a language for sharing text electronically. The world already knew about the internet as a way for computers to communicate with each other, but Tim Berners-Lee dreamt of combining the idea of the internet with hypertext and making it available* for everyone and easier to use.

After experimenting with different ideas and trying out different methods, he worked out a way to do it and in 1990, with the help of Robert Cailliau, he produced the first version of the World Wide Web, the first web browser and the first web server. It went online in 1991.

In 1994, Berners-Lee founded W3C (World Wide Web Consortium) at the Laboratory of Computer Science (LCS) at the Massachusetts Institute of Technology (MIT) in Boston. This is an organisation that tries to improve the world wide web. He could have tried to make a lot of money out of his invention, but he decided to make the world wide web widely available to everyone without asking for payment*. Now hundreds of millions of people are using it and it has become part of our daily lives.

In spite of the size and importance of his invention, Berners-Lee is not rich. He's not very materialistic and for many years he was happy to drive a 13-year-old car. He enjoys being in nature and wants to protect it.

He has received many awards for his work. In 2004, the Queen made him a "Sir" and, in 2011, he received the Mikhail Gorbachev Award for "The Man Who Changed the World".

VOCABULARY: ***available** – verfügbar; **payment** – Bezahlung

		T	F
1	Tim Berners-Lee is an American information expert.	☐	☐
2	In the early 1980s, Tim Berners-Lee worked in Switzerland.	☐	☐
3	He discovered a way of using hypertext to exchange information.	☐	☐
4	He experimented with the idea of combining hypertext with the internet.	☐	☐
5	The first web browser went online in 1994.	☐	☐
6	Tim Berners-Lee dreamt of becoming a millionaire via the internet.	☐	☐
7	He wanted everyone in the world to enjoy using his invention.	☐	☐
8	Tim Berners-Lee liked to buy a new car every year.	☐	☐
9	In 2004, he became Sir Tim Berners-Lee.	☐	☐
10	He received the Mikhail Gorbachev Award for changing the world with his invention.	☐	☐

nach SB p. 67

1 Read the dialogue and complete it with the words and phrases from the box.

inventions	worked out	try it out	experimented	discovered	improved
designed	find	wheelchair	produce	ramp	entered

A trip to the Science Museum

Friday, on the telephone

Brian Hi, Sandie. Guess what? I'm going to the Science Museum tomorrow. I [1].. a competition for people with disabilities and I've won a free trip to London. They're sending a special bus with a [2].. for my [3].. . The trip is for two people. Would you like to come with me?

Sandie Yes, sure. Great idea. I'd love to. I've never been to the Science Museum.

Brian Super. The bus is picking me up here at 9 o'clock. I'm looking forward to seeing all those fantastic [4].. !

Sandie Me, too. I'll come round to your place at eight thirty. OK?

Brian Great. See you then.

Saturday morning, on the way to the Science Museum

Brian I've got an information brochure here. There's so much to see. Where do we start?

Sandie What about there: 'Making the Modern World'?

Brian Yeah, we can see some incredible objects there, I'm sure. I'd like to [5].. the very first steam locomotive* and see how it works.

Sandie Do you know who [6].. steam power?

Brian Yes, a man called James Watt. Everyone knows that. And the first steam locomotive …

Sandie … was 'The Rocket'. A man called Robert Stephenson built it in 1829.

Brian It's here in the museum. Maybe we can [7].. ?

Sandie I don't think so, but look! There are other things you can use – like early computers.

Brian Well, I know modern computers are incredible machines, but I like to think about the very first ones. Who [8].. them? Who [9].. how to make them?

Sandie Well, it says here: there was a man called Babbage in the 1880s who [10].. with a machine he called his 'Difference Engine'. We can go and see that.

Brian It's amazing to think the idea of a computer is so old when you see the numbers of smartphones, laptops and tablets the big companies [11].. these days. Things have [12].. over the last 150 years.

Sandie Well, all good ideas have to start somewhere, don't they? And it was a very good idea to ask me to come with you today! I can't wait to get there.

VOCABULARY: *steam locomotive – Dampflokomotive

nach SB p. 70

1 **Look at exercise 4 on page 67 of your Student's Book again. Imagine that you, too, have invented something: maybe a robot, or a new machine, or an app for smartphones. Choose one and write about what it can do, how you came up with the idea and how you designed and improved it. Write 120–180 words.**

Start like this:

My new invention

I've invented something. It's a ...

1 Read what Joe, a boy from Canada, says about his life. Then tick T (*True*) or F (*False*).

My family and I, we're Mennonites. I have two older sisters and a younger brother. I go to a public high school in Toronto and I think I have quite a normal life – just like any other 13-year-old boy. I'm in my school's swimming team and at the weekends we usually go to competitions which are held at other high schools.

Sometimes I'm really glad that my parents aren't strict Mennonites. But my uncle, my aunt and their children are. My cousin Sam is as old as I am. We come from the same family, but his life is completely different from mine. They, too, are a large family, with six children. We don't see them very often. They live on a small farm in the country, not far from our place. It's nice there. They have horses and lots of other animals. My cousins don't go to school. My aunt and uncle teach them at home. Being a strict Mennonite also means working really hard. They get up very early in the morning and then all my cousins help with the work on the farm – they feed the animals, work in the fields and my aunt's vegetable garden and do the cooking. The girls make the family's clothes and keep the house tidy while the boys help my uncle. He's a carpenter* and makes furniture*. They don't have a car but a horse-drawn carriage*.

I wouldn't like to be a strict Mennonite. It's hard to imagine a life without electricity. Just think of that: no TV, no phone, no computer games, no cars! And I would also miss my friends at school and my swimming team, of course.

VOCABULARY
***carpenter** – Tischler/in, Zimmermann; **furniture** – Möbel; **horse-drawn carriage** – Pferdekutsche

		T	F
1	Joe goes to a public high school and is a member of the swimming team.	☐	☐
2	He comes from a family of strict Mennonites and has got three brothers.	☐	☐
3	His cousin Sam lives on a farm and Joe often talks to him at school.	☐	☐
4	His cousins work hard on their farm and aren't allowed to get up late.	☐	☐
5	On the farm the boys help with the cooking and the housework.	☐	☐
6	Joe's uncle works as a carpenter and owns two carriages and a car.	☐	☐

nach SB p. 76

1 Look at the pictures. What are the teenagers allowed (✔) or not allowed (✘) to do? Write sentences.

buy own clothes	take the dog for a walk	ski here
play video games	~~go roller-skating without pads~~	draw on the board
play basketball	go to the disco	

✘

1 He isn't allowed to go roller-skating without pads.

✘

2 ....

✔

3 ....

✘

4 ....

✔

5 ....

✘

6 ....

✔

7 ....

✘

8 ....

nach SB p. 78

1 **Ask a friend the following questions. Write down her/his answers. Then write a report (100–120 words) about what she/he told you.**

Questions for your interview:

Do your parents let you ... / Are you allowed to ...

- *... dye your hair?*
- *... get a nose stud?*
- *... only wear black clothes?*
- *... get a tattoo?*
- *... stay up late?*
- *... hang out with your friends (at the shopping centre, the cinema, etc.)?*
- *... make a mess in your room?*
- *... go out without telling your parents where you go?*
- *... invite your friends every day?*
- *... surf the internet as long as you want to?*

....

....

....

....

....

....

....

....

....

....

....

....

....

....

....

....

....

nach SB p. 79

1 **Look at the picture and read the short text. Then write what Ryan's mum told him after the party. Use *be allowed to* in your sentences.**

The party

Ryan's parents went away for the weekend. They wanted to visit Ryan's grandmother and planned to be back Sunday evening. Ryan didn't want to join them, so he said that he would stay at his best friend Nick's place. Their parents said it was OK. But Ryan and Nick had a plan: they called their friends and invited them to a party at Ryan's house. The party was great, until Ryan's parents turned up! A neighbour had phoned them and told them what was going on at their house …

Start like this:

Ryan, you know that you aren't allowed to have a party when we're away. Why didn't you stay at Nick's house? We can't believe you any more! And you know that your friends aren't allowed to … and of course they aren't allowed to …

....

....

....

....

....

....

....

....

....

nach SB p. 79

1 Complete the sentences with *could(n't)* or *was(n't)/were(n't) able.*

1 All the kids signed a petition and .... to stop the plans for a new car park.

2 Mr Parker .... to come up with a good solution at the end of the meeting.

3 We went to the beach, but we .... to pick up all the litter there.

4 I'm sorry I .... come to the party last night – I was ill.

5 Before 1897, girls .... study at a university in Austria.

6 In 1897, a woman .... to become the first female medical doctor in Austria.

7 Women in Austria .... vote until 1918.

8 In 1956, a lady called Rosa Parks .... to change the law about seats on buses in America.

9 Before 1956, African-Americans .... use the same seats on buses as white people.

10 Erin Brockovich and her lawyer .... to win a lot of money for the people of Hinkley.

2 Complete the answers to the questions using the correct form of *have(n't)/has(n't) been able to.*

1 Has Sandra done anything to help since she heard the news about the park?
Yes, she .... find out more about the plans for a car park.

2 What have Sandra and Richard done to try and save the park?
They .... talk to a city planner.

3 Did Mr Parker come up with a solution to the problem?
No, he .... find one yet.

4 Can you tell me if Mary has finished her homework?
No, she .... finish it yet.

5 Have you bought the tickets for the concert on Saturday?
Yes, I .... get four fantastic seats.

6 Are you still going to buy that new car?
No, we .... save enough money.

7 Are Peter and Lisa happy in their new house?
I don't know. I .... visit them for weeks.

8 Can we go swimming this afternoon?
No, they .... clean up all the plastic from the beach yet.

1 **Belinda lives on the coast in Texas. The beaches in her area are polluted* and she would like to do something about it. She has decided to organise a petition to the city council. First she writes a letter to the council and describes the beach and says what she wants to do about it. Use the words in the box to write her letter (120–180 words).**

VOCABULARY: ***polluted** – verschmutzt

- Her plans: wants to save the animals, clean up the beach, collect the litter etc.
- She asks for: helpers, signs: Keep our beaches clean! (she needs money for this)

Belinda's petition

....

....

....

....

....

....

....

....

....

....

....

....

....

....

....

....

....

nach SB p. 86

1 Read the text and answer the questions below.

On December 1st, 1955, police in Montgomery, Alabama, arrested Rosa Parks because she refused to give up her seat to a white man on the bus. Her arrest led to* a 381-day bus boycott. At that time African-Americans living in the south of the US didn't have the same rights as white people – they weren't allowed to go to the same schools, restaurants or theatres as white people.
On the night of Rosa Parks' arrest many African-Americans met in front of churches and in the streets to organise their protest. One of them was Martin Luther King Jr., a young priest. One of his heroes was Mahatma Gandhi. Martin Luther King Jr. organised peaceful demonstrations and fought for the rights of African-Americans in a non-violent way.
There were marches, meetings and sit-ins: African-Americans went into restaurants for white people and just sat there for a long time to protest against the situation. Nobody served* them any food or drinks and usually the police would come and arrest them. But sit-ins became more and more popular and many people took part in them.
In 1963 Martin Luther King Jr. organised the March on Washington and more than 200,000 black and white people joined him. The famous speech he gave there was called "I have a dream". In this speech he spoke about his hopes for the future, that black and white people would have the same rights one day and would be able to live together peacefully. In 1964, Martin Luther King Jr. won the Nobel Peace Prize and a year later, African-Americans finally got the right to vote. Martin Luther King Jr. was shot in 1968. Today people in the US celebrate Martin Luther King Day on January 20th, his birthday, to remember his courageous* fight.

VOCABULARY: ***led to** – führte zu; **serve** – servieren; **courageous** – mutig

1 What happened when Rosa Parks refused to give up her seat?

....

2 Why did African-Americans in the south of the US protest?

....

3 What did Martin Luther King Jr. organise?

....

4 What is a sit-in?

....

5 What was his famous speech about?

....

6 What do people in the US celebrate each year?

....

  nach SB p. 89

1 What will/won't James be able to do? Write sentences.

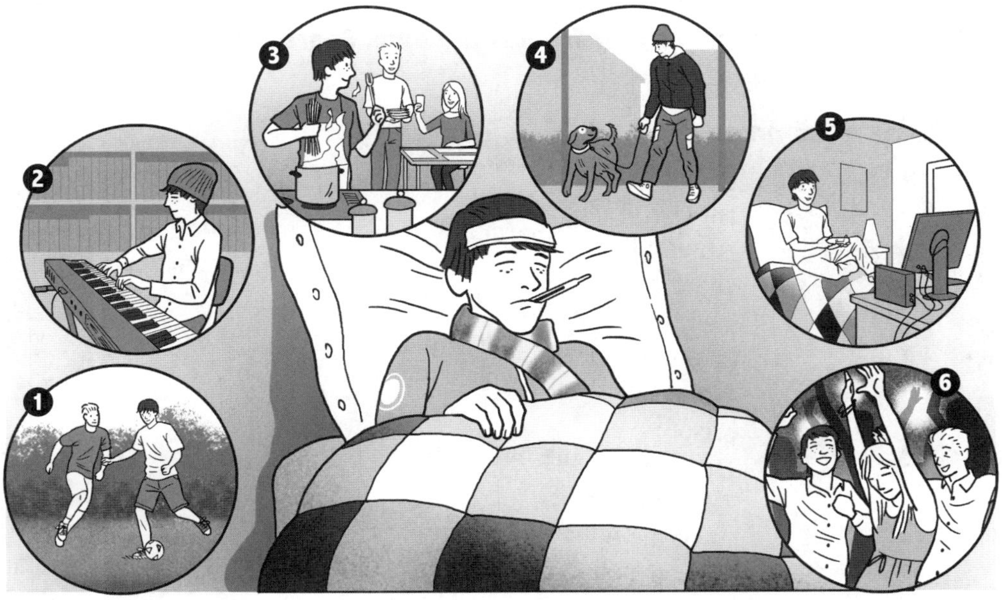

1 ....

2 ....

3 ....

4 ....

5 ....

6 ....

2 Fill in the correct forms of *(not) be able to.*

1 When the ship sank, they .... rescue the people on board, but they .... find their bags and suitcases.

2 Sue broke her right arm, so she .... do the Maths test tomorrow.

3 I forgot my key at school. That's why I .... open the door right now. I'll have to wait for Mum.

4 I .... find my camera last week, so I'll have to buy a new one.

5 The city council .... solve the problem yet. They are still trying to find a solution.

6 With the money they collected at their school last year they .... save some trees in the rainforest.

1 **Have a look at the leaflet. Imagine that you are spending a holiday in San Francisco, California. Choose three or four things from the leaflet and write about these places in an email (100–120 words) to one of your friends at home. Search the internet for more information on these places.**

Welcome to San Francisco!

San Francisco welcomes you!
Visit the amazing sights of San Francisco:
Enjoy the fantastic view from Coit Tower!
Go for a walk in Chinatown!
Visit one of the shops or restaurants in Fisherman's Wharf!
Feed the sea lions at Pier 39!
Take a boat ride to Alcatraz and explore the island which was a prison!
Drive across the famous Golden Gate Bridge!
Visit the Aquarium of the Bay and have a look at the sharks there!
Ride the hills of the city in the world-famous cable cars*!

Welcome to San Francisco!

VOCABULARY
***cable car** – Straßenbahn, die von einem Drahtseil gezogen wird

1 **Here's an interview with Alessandro, an Italian boy who is spending a year as an exchange student* in Carmel, California. Write the verbs in the present perfect continuous.**

(**A** = Alessandro, **I** = Interviewer)

I Alessandro, how long [1].. (you / live) in California?

A I [2].. (live) here for three months now. I arrived in January.

I And do you like living here?

A It's great and it's so different from the place where I come from, a small town in northern Italy.

I How long [3].. (you / learn) English?

A For three years now. But my English is getting better and better because I go to school here and I often hang out with my friends from school.

I [4].. (you / explore) California a bit?

A Yes, my host family* and I often go away at weekends. I've been to Los Angeles, San Diego, Palm Springs. California is a great place!

I What's it like to live with an American family?

A My host parents are really friendly and I get along really well with Jake and Jenny, their kids. I've got a big room for myself and I often invite friends from school. My parents flew over to see me from Italy. I [5].. (already / miss) them a lot.

I How long [6].. (they / stay) with you?

A For a week. They will go back to Italy in four days.

I Thanks for talking to us, Alessandro! And enjoy your stay here!

VOCABULARY
***exchange student** – Austauschstudent/in;
host family – Gastfamilie

nach SB p. 95

1 **Read the text and look at the picture. Continue the story (120–180 words). What happened to Patricia and Jeff? Also give your story a title.**

A trip through Death Valley

Patricia and her boyfriend Jeff were travelling through Death Valley. They left the hotel early in the morning because they knew it would be a very hot day. The weather report said that the temperature would go up to 50 °C, but Jeff wanted to take photos of the desert. They were driving along the dirt road when suddenly they heard a strange noise. Jeff stopped the car immediately. When they got out, they saw the flat tyre*.

VOCABULARY
***flat tyre** – Platten

....

....

....

....

....

....

....

....

....

....

....

....

....

....

....

....

....

nach SB p. 95

1 **Put the verbs in brackets into the present perfect continuous. Circle *since* or *for*. Then match the sentences with the pictures.**

1 Sandra is a good driver. She .... (drive) *since* / *for* eight years.

2 Christine .... (wait) in the desert *since* / *for* three hours. She is thirsty and has a terrible headache.

3 Alan and Keira .... (play) computer games *since* / *for* 3 o'clock in the afternoon. They look really tired now.

4 I .... (try) to do my Maths homework *since* / *for* two hours, but I haven't been able to finish it yet.

5 Mrs Andrews .... (work) as a doctor at the hospital *since* / *for* six months.

6 Tim and his friends .... (swim) in the lake *since* / *for* an hour.

7 Olivia and Claire decided to leave England and *since* / *for* last year, they .... (live) in California.

8 I .... (learn) to speak Spanish *since* / *for* 2017. I hope to visit Spain next year.

1 Complete the sentences with the present simple passive of the words in brackets and fill in the missing words from the box.

forest fire
tsunami
volcano
avalanches

1 A .... happens when there is an undersea earthquake.
The coast .... (hit) by huge waves.

2 .... are thousands of tons of snow coming down a mountain. It is very difficult for the rescue teams to save people who .... (trap) under the snow.

3 In a .... many animals .... (kill) and many trees .... (destroy) by the fire.

4 When a .... erupts, the surrounding* area .... (cover) in lava and ashes. People .... (often warn) by scientists and evacuated.

VOCABULARY: *surrounding – umliegend

nach SB p. 106

1 **Read the article about the fires in Australia. Then answer the questions below.**

Early in February 2009 Australia was hit by the worst fire disaster in the country's history. The fire destroyed large parts of the forest and bush in the southeastern state of Victoria and spread* quickly north of the state's capital Melbourne. Before the fires broke out, the weather was unusually hot with temperatures in the 40s.

The fires destroyed many houses and left thousands of people without homes. More than 200 people died because they were trapped by the fire before they could get out. Unfortunately, rescue teams were not able to help them. Firefighters* from all over the country were flown in to help fight the fire. They worked day and night. But the fires couldn't be controlled because of the heat and the strong winds.

Some places, such as the small town of Marysville, were trapped in the fire and completely destroyed. Only 12 out of 200 houses were still standing when the fire was finally extinguished*. Some residents* returned to their homes to look around after the fire. All the buildings in town were destroyed. The post office was gone and their school was also burnt to the ground. More than 100 people, from a town of just 550, were killed in the fires. One man managed to survive in his basement*. He had stored* food and water there. His car, which was parked in the garage, melted because of the heat of the fires. It is a miracle that he survived.

Police believe that arsonists* started some of the fires. But because of the very hot weather, the fires could have been the result of lightning, too.

VOCABULARY
***spread** – sich ausbreiten; **firefighter** – Feuerwehrmann/frau; **extinguish** – löschen; **resident** – Einwohner/in; **basement** – Keller; **store** – lagern; **arsonist** – Brandstifter/in

1 Where did the fires break out?

....

2 How many people lost their lives?

....

3 Why were the firefighters not able to stop the fires?

....

4 What happened to the small town of Marysville?

....

5 How did one man survive the fire at his home?

....

6 Why did the fires start?

....

nach SB p. 103

1 **Read Steven's report. Complete the text with the past simple passive form of the verbs in brackets.**

How I survived a tornado

"Last year, as I was travelling through Nevada in my car, I [1].. (surprise) by a tornado. There was a tornado warning on the radio. I was in the middle of the desert and there was no way to escape the tornado. The advice on the radio was to leave the car and lie down flat on the ground. So I parked my car quickly and got out. I could see the tornado coming right at me! I covered my head and tried to stay calm. With a terrible noise my car [2].. (hit) by the tornado.

I [3].. (lift) off the ground. When I opened my eyes again after some minutes, the tornado had gone. My car [4].. (crush). I couldn't move because my legs [5].. (injure). Half an hour later another car drove by. The driver stopped immediately and called an ambulance.

I [6].. (take) to hospital and had to stay there for three days. Some buildings [7].. (destroy) by the tornado too. I'm really glad that I survived and I' I never forget the sight of that huge tornado coming straight towards me."

nach SB p. 106

1 **Use the picture to write the story about Claire who was trapped in an avalanche. Write 120–180 words.**

Rescued by a dog

....

....

....

....

....

....

....

....

....

....

....

....

....

....

....

....

....

1 **Put the verbs in brackets into the correct form. Use the 2nd conditional.**

Castaway

1 If my plane .... (crash) into the ocean, I .... (start) swimming.

2 If I .... (reach) a desert island, I .... (explore) the island first.

3 I .... (eat) berries if I .... (be) hungry.

4 If I .... (have) a knife with me, I .... (cut down) branches and build a hut.

5 I .... (light) a fire if I .... (have) some matches.

6 If I .... (feel) lonely, I .... (talk) to myself but I .... (not give up).

7 If I .... (see) a ship, I .... (wave) at it and shout loudly.

8 If the people .... (spot) me on the island, I .... (be) saved.

nach SB p. 115

1 **a Continue the story (40–70 words). What happened next? What did Lisa do?**

The new boy at school

There was a new boy at Hannah's school. His name was Toby and all the girls liked him. They thought that he was the cutest boy in the school. Hannah's best friend Lisa thought so, too. She couldn't help looking at Toby during the lunch breaks in the school cafeteria. But Hannah was not interested in him. One day after school, Hannah went to the café for an ice cream. It was a hot day – and guess who was standing in front of her? Toby. They started to talk a bit about school and then they went for a walk through the park with their ice creams. Lisa lived near the park. When she saw Toby and Hannah from the window of her room, she couldn't believe her eyes. How could Hannah do that to her? ...

....

....

....

....

....

....

b What would you do if you were Lisa? Write a short paragraph.

....

....

....

....

....

....

nach SB p. 112

1 **Imagine the following situations. How would people react? Finish the sentences.**

What would the people say?

1 What would your parents say if you forgot to feed your hamster?

If I forgot to feed my hamster, my parents ...

2 How would your teachers react if you fell asleep during a lesson?

....

3 What would your friends say if you dyed your hair green?

....

4 What would your mum say if you got a tattoo?

....

5 How would your teachers react if you took a pet rat to school?

....

2 **Imagine the following situations. Then finish the sentences. Say what is true for you.**

What would you do if ...?

1 If a good friend forgot my birthday, ...

....

2 If my best friend didn't keep a secret, ...

....

3 If I found a gold necklace in front of school, ...

....

4 If I was late for school and had a test in the first lesson, ...

....

5 If two older boys bullied* me and took my things, ...

....

6 If my friends wanted to play a nasty trick on someone, ...

....

VOCABULARY
***bully** – tyrannisieren

nach SB p. 113

1 **Imagine it's your lucky day. Choose three situations. Then write *if*-sentences about what you would do. Write two sentences for each situation.**

- ✓ You won the jackpot in the lottery.
- ✓ You could go to California tomorrow.
- ✓ You could move to your favourite place.
- ✓ You could give a huge party.

Example: If I went to California tomorrow, I'd visit Universal Studios in Hollywood.

....

....

....

....

....

....

....

....

2 **Imagine you sent an email to the wrong person. In your email you criticised a boy called Thomas. You didn't send it to your friend Tim, but to Thomas! Write what you would do (100–120 words).**

....

....

....

....

....

....

....

....

....

....

....

....

....

1 Put the verbs in brackets into the correct form. Use the 2nd conditional.

1 I love adventure trips. If I .... (have) a month off, I .... (fly) to Botswana.

2 If my plane .... (land) in Gaborone, I .... (visit) a museum and then I .... (fly) to Maun.

3 I .... (go) to the Okavango Delta if I .... (travel) across the country.

4 If I .... (hire) a car, I .... (drive) through the desert.

5 I .... (take) a guide with me if this .... (be) safer than travelling alone.

6 If I .... (see) wild animals, I .... (take) lots of pictures or I .... (try) to film them with my camera.

7 I .... (not get) too close to them if there .... (be) elephants, leopards or other big animals.

Go on. Write three more sentences about what you would do if you had a chance to go to Botswana.

....

....

....

....

....

....

nach SB p. 121

1 **In an article for his school magazine Oliver writes about some of the wild animals he saw in Botswana. Look at the texts in your Student's Book again. Use the information in the box and write a text (120–180 words) about what we can do to protect wildlife.**

Animals in danger

- crime to kill wild animals
- in danger
- not buy animal products
- not buy leopard or tiger skins
- not buy ivory and coral necklaces or jewellery, handbags or shoes made of alligator or snake skin
- illegal to take wildlife souvenirs back to your country

....

....

....

....

....

....

....

....

....

....

....

....

....

nach SB p. 118

1 **What are you going to do in the holidays? Write sentences. Use *(not) be going to.***

Example:
I: spend a week at the seaside.*
In the holidays I'm going to spend a week at the seaside.
Or: In the holidays I'm not going to spend a week at the seaside.

my friends and I: lie in the sun all day

....

we: stay up late

....

we: go to lots of parties

....

my family: go to another country by plane *(say which country in your sentence)*

....

I: speak English

....

I: read lots of books

....

my friends and I: watch lots of DVDs

....

I: enter a sports competition *(say which kind of sport in your sentence)*

....

I: tidy my room

....

I: study for school

....

VOCABULARY
***at the seaside** – am Meer

nach SB p. 122

1 **Imagine that you are one of the tourists in the picture. You are spending three weeks in the Kruger National Park in South Africa. Your guide promised you some good photos of the "Big Five". Back at the camp you send an email to a friend. Tell her/him about the exciting trip, the amazing animals you spotted and the night you spent in the wilderness.**
Write the email (100–120 words).

A trip through Kruger National Park

Kruger National Park is one of the largest and oldest parks and game reserves* in South Africa. The park covers 18,989 square km. It is huge – 350 km from north to south and 60 km from east to west.

VOCABULARY: *game reserve – Wildtierreservat

....

....

....

....

....

....

....

....

....

....

....

....

....

Playing for others

On January 12th 1918 a classical music concert took place in the Konzerthaus in Vienna. The money from the ticket sales went to help the families of the Austrian and Hungarian soldiers who died in the First World War. It was the first example of a benefit concert.

The Concert for Bangladesh

The concert in Vienna was small. Not many people outside of Austria learnt about it. In the 1960s television helped to make pop music extremely popular all over the world. Of course, benefit concerts started to get much bigger audiences* too.

The first modern-day example took place on August 1st 1971 when ex-Beatle George Harrison organised *The Concert for Bangladesh*. Harrison invited famous friends – musicians such as Bob Dylan, Ringo Starr and Ravi Shankar – to join him on stage at Madison Square Garden in New York. Money from the concert went to help refugees from East Pakistan. Harrison made a best-selling live album of the music and a documentary film about the concert for cinemas all over the world.

Live Aid*

In 1985 Bob Geldof, singer of the Irish band *The Boomtown Rats*, saw a news report about Ethiopia. He was shocked to see how thousands were dying of hunger and wanted to do something to help. He decided to organise a benefit concert in London. But his plans got bigger and bigger, and finally two concerts took place on the same day – one at Wembley Stadium in London, the other at the JFK Stadium in Philadelphia. On July 13th 72,000 people in London and 100,000 in Philadelphia watched artists such as *The Who*, *Queen*, Paul McCartney, *U2* and David Bowie sing on stage. But far more people – an amazing number of 1.9 billion people in 150 different countries – watched the concerts live on TV. One musician, Phil Collins, wanted to do as much as possible to help. He played in London, and then quickly got on a plane to the US so he could play in Philadelphia too. The Live Aid concerts and the hit single "Do They Know It's Christmas?" raised a lot of money – $245 million.

America: A Tribute to Heroes*

On September 11th 2001, there was a terrible terrorist attack in New York. Terrorists flew planes into the Twin Tower buildings killing more than 2,500 people. Only ten days after the tragedy actor George Clooney organised a telethon, a TV concert to raise money. People watched famous singers and actors on TV and then phoned in to donate* money. The singers of the show included Bruce Springsteen, Sting, Celine Dion and Mariah Carey. Other famous actors and sports people such as Tom Hanks, Muhammad Ali, Cameron Diaz and Tom Cruise were there to speak and ask for money. Many of the stars also helped answer the phones and take the donations*. A lot of TV stations showed the concert. The show raised over $200 million. The money went to help the families of firefighters and policemen that died in the terrorist attacks.

Big and small

Benefit concerts don't need famous people to help out. Every year many smaller concerts take place all over the world. Local bands and musicians bring people together and ask them to donate money. The power of music gets people to help others everywhere.

VOCABULARY: ***audience** – Publikum; **aid** – Hilfe; **heroes** – Helden, Heldinnen; **donate** – spenden; **donation** – (Geld-)Spende

SB p. 8

James Holman: the record traveller

"He had eyes in his mouth, eyes in his nose, eyes in his ears, and eyes in his mind." – William Jerdan

James Holman lived more than a hundred and fifty years ago. He travelled more than 400,000 km – further than anyone before him. And in those days travelling long distances was hard, even for fit people.

But James Holman wasn't fit. He was blind, and he was ill. He suffered from rheumatism. He was in so much pain that it was often difficult for him to get out of bed in the morning. But every morning he grabbed his walking stick to go for long walks.

Born in Exeter in the south of England in 1786, James was a healthy boy, and it was his dream to see the world. At the age of twelve, he joined the Royal Navy*. Soon he was on board a ship sailing across the Atlantic, towards the coast of Canada, working very hard.

Life at sea was brutal. The freezing, wet weather was very bad for his health. He started to feel terrible pains in his bones. His feet hurt so badly that walking became difficult for him. He stayed in the Royal Navy until 1810. Then they sent him back to England. By the time he was twenty-five, he was unable to walk, and he was completely blind too.

In those days, blind people had extremely hard lives. Most of them ended up in the streets, begging for money. Not Holman. He got himself a metal walking stick. Listening carefully to the tap tap tap that came from the stick, he started to explore the streets of London, all alone. He was blind, but he learnt to 'see' using his ears.

A few years later he went on his first journey, to France. The roads were awful. The coaches were over-crowded with people. Holman didn't speak a word of French. Nobody spoke English. The blind man was all alone – but starting to travel was the best decision in Holman's life! His health became better and he felt great.

Holman became very good at finding his way around strange cities, tap-tap-tapping his way, noticing the sounds and smells of streets and market places. People asked him how a blind man could enjoy sightseeing. He said, "Being blind doesn't stop me from enjoying travelling. It makes me more curious. I can't see, but I can hear. I can feel. I can smell and I can taste."

His next trip was to Italy. He became the first blind person to reach the top of Mount Vesuvius – an active volcano at that time. Back in England, Holman started to write. Two of his books became very successful and he became famous. Now he could go on a journey around the world.

The adventures of the blind man were amazing. In Brazil he visited a gold mine. In South Africa he taught himself to ride a horse. In Ceylon he took part in an elephant hunt. He crossed Zanzibar and Tasmania on foot. And in China a swarm of wasps* attacked him – a very painful experience. But he never gave up. He lived his big dream – his dream to 'see' the world.

VOCABULARY: *navy – Marine; **wasp** – Wespe

Mary Kingsley: a Victorian lady in Africa

Mary Kingsley was born in North London in 1862. When she was a girl, her mother became quite ill, and her father was never at home. So Mary had to look after her mother and had little time to go to school. But while she was looking after her mother, she studied physics, chemistry, biology and maths on her own. She learned Latin and German too.

Mary had a big dream. She wanted to see the world. She wanted to be an explorer. She wanted to travel to Africa. When both her parents died in 1891, she wanted to start travelling. That was not easy because in the 19th century women did not usually travel alone. But that didn't stop Mary Kingsley. Mary made two long African journeys, one in 1893 and one in 1895. There are many wild stories about her travels.

On her first journey she went to Angola, Congo, Cameroon and Nigeria. She lived with the people in their huts and she ate their food. And Mary always dressed in black from head to toe. In the middle of the wilderness she looked like a lady going to a tea party!

She collected rare* fish for the British Museum, and she had quite a few dangerous adventures. Once she heard some noise outside her tent; it was a leopard; she threw a water jug* at it and it ran away. And when some hippos blocked her way, she hit them with her umbrella. Once a crocodile tried to climb into her boat. She hit it with her paddle so it gave up and went back into the water.

In 1895 she went where no white woman had ever been before. She went to see the Fang people who were cannibals. The Fang were quite friendly, but one night Mary found a bag with a human hand, three big toes, four eyes, and two ears in her tent. She also wanted to climb Mount Cameroon (4,040 metres). She had to do that alone, because the men with her were too weak* to get to the top.

Finally, Mary went back to England. She wrote two bestsellers (*Travels in West Africa* and *West African Studies*). In her books, she criticised the Europeans, especially the missionaries, for destroying so much of the African culture. Mary returned to Africa in 1899 and worked in a hospital for typhoid* patients. She got typhoid herself and died on June 3rd, 1900. She was one of the great female* explorers of the 19th century.

VOCABULARY: ***rare** – seltene/r/s; **jug** – Krug; **weak** – schwach; **typhoid** – Typhus; **female** – weiblich

Candyman

SCENE 1

Ana, Nick and Dan are on a school trip in the countryside. They are sitting around a late-night campfire.

Ana That's just silly. Of course, it's not true.

Nick Are you sure? Why don't you try it?

Ana Because I don't want to. What do you think Dan? Dan!

Dan What … ? What … ? I'm sorry. I think I fell asleep for a few minutes. What are you talking about?

Ana Nick says that if you look into a mirror and say "Candyman" three times, an evil spirit will appear in front of you.

Nick Yes, and then he leaves the mirror to come and … GET YOU!

Ana Stop it, Nick. It's not funny.

Dan Don't listen to him, Ana. He just wants to scare you.

Ana So it's not true.

Dan Of course not. It's just a silly superstition like if you break a mirror it brings you seven years' bad luck.

Ana Or if you see a rainbow, you can make a wish.

Dan Exactly. Those wishes never come true, do they?

Nick They do if you wish for something bad but no one ever does that.

Dan Oh, Nick. Don't talk nonsense!

SCENE 2

Mr Wallis, the teacher, arrives and sits down beside them.

Mr Wallis Listen, everyone. We've got a big day tomorrow. I want everyone up and having breakfast by 7 a.m.

Dan OK, I'm going to bed then.

Nick Me too. Goodnight.

Mr Wallis Goodnight and remember, be careful what you dream about.

Ana What do you mean?

Mr Wallis They say that whatever* you dream about in a new bed comes true.

Dan Mr Wallis! You're worse than Nick.

SCENE 3

Nick is in his sleeping bag. He is dreaming.

Nick Wow, this house is really spooky. Who lives here?

Ana A ghost, a spirit by the name of Candyman.

Nick What? I can't believe it.

Ana So, Nick. There's the mirror. Now say "Candyman". Say it three times. Nice and loud.

Nick Don't be silly. I'm not doing that.

Ana Why not? Are you scared? Do it.

Dan Do it.

Mr Wallis Do it.

Nick Oh, alright. Candyman. Is that OK?

Ana And again.

Nick Candyman. Happy now?

Dan And one more time.

Nick CANDYMAN!

VOCABULARY: ***whatever** – was auch immer

SCENE 4

It's the next morning. Dan is sitting eating his breakfast. Ana joins him with a tray of food.

Ana Hi, Dan, can I join you?

Dan Of course you can.

Ana And did you sleep well?

Dan Yes, very well. I really didn't want to get up this morning.

Ana And did your dreams come true, Dan?

Dan Did my dreams come true? I'm not sure what you mean.

Ana Don't you remember, before we went to bed last night. Mr Wallis said that dreams in a new bed always come true.

Dan Oh yes, I remember. But I can't remember any dreams. What about you?

Ana Well, I think I dreamed about Nick. He went missing and no one could find him. It was very strange.

Dan Well, he's not here yet. Maybe your dream has come true. Spooky.

Ana Stop it. I'm worried. Maybe we should go and look for him.

Dan Oh alright. I'll go and look for him after breakfast.

SCENE 5

Dan and Ana meet outside the camp washrooms.

Ana Any luck?

Dan No. There's no sign of him anywhere.

Ana I'm starting to get really worried.

Dan Don't be silly. You know Nick. It's just one of his silly jokes.

Ana But Mr Wallis wants us all ready to go in five minutes.

Dan He'll be here. I promise you. Now if you'll excuse me.

Ana Where are you going?

Dan In here. I'm just going to wash my face and brush my teeth.

SCENE 6

Dan is in the washroom brushing his teeth.

Dan Because I'm happy … happy … h.a.p.p.y. … happy …

Voice Help me. Help.

Dan What! Who's that? Who's there?

Voice It's me, Dan. Nick. It's Nick.

Dan Nick? Nick, is that you? Where are you?

Voice I'm here Dan. I'm right in front of you. Look.

Dan What does he mean, right in front of me. There's nothing but a mirror in front of … Oh my God! Nick – what happened?

Alessia

I've been friends with Alessia for two years now. When she and her family moved here, I wasn't really happy at first. A girl from a foreign country – so it would be difficult to talk to her. "She still has to learn the language", Mum said. "George, you must help her." "Why me?" I said. "I've never done anything like that. I'm not a teacher. All I can do is teach her how to play football." "Don't be silly", Mum said. "And take her some of your old books, the simple ones. And some of your soft toys too." "Mum!" I cried, "I've had those books for years. I like them. And the soft toys too. I've had them since I was a baby."

I knew my mum. So I did as she told me; I took the stuff and said hello to the family. They seemed really happy, and Alessia smiled and smiled – but didn't say a word.

"You've been a great help", Mum said when I came back. "Now let's see what else we can do for them."

From then on it was like this:
Mum: Take this MP3-player to Alessia!
Me: But ...
Mum: No but, you haven't used it for years, you listen to your music on your mobile phone anyway.

Anyway, again and again I went next door, and of course, I talked to Alessia about this and that. And I kind of liked the way she smiled when she got these presents. And I liked the cookies* her mum gave me.

Then one day a kid was making fun of her at school and I stepped in*. Some of the kids laughed at me for that, but I didn't really mind. After all I am the school's best footballer, so nobody would give me a hard time.

Anyway, what happened was that Alessia and I became friends. Just like that, I think. We talked to each other every day and spent some time together. I quite liked talking to her, and I also noticed that her English got much better. For some time her parents kept saying, "You've been such a big help, George, thank you very much". But then they stopped because they began to understand that I quite liked helping her. And I actually like Alessia, too. There's only one little problem now. Her parents are talking about moving to another city. And Alessia and me are now talking about how we can stop them.

VOCABULARY: ***cookies** – Kekse; **step in** – eingreifen, dazwischen gehen

Nikola Tesla: The man who invented* the 20th century

Nikola Tesla was a Serbian-Austrian. When he arrived in New York in June 1884 he only had 4 cents in his pocket. When he died alone on January 7th 1943 in room 3327 of the Hotel New Yorker, he had no money at all.

In the 59 years between those two dates, Tesla made some of the most important inventions of the 20th century. He invented the electric motor, fluorescent light bulbs, neon signs, the first remote-controlled boat and the first speedometer for cars. He also designed the world's first hydroelectric power plant* at Niagara Falls, which used the power of the water to produce electricity.

So why wasn't Tesla a billionaire when he died?

Perhaps it was his most important invention that was also the reason for his bad luck. In the late 1880s Tesla invented AC electrical current*, a new kind of electricity. It was cheaper than the DC electrical current* that people used at the time. But Thomas Edison, perhaps the most famous inventor of the time, had all his money invested* in DC current. So he was against AC current. He told people that it was very dangerous. In 1893 at the World Exposition in Chicago, Tesla went on stage. He wanted to show people that it was OK to use AC current. He passed a huge current through his body to power up* light bulbs.

Tesla had to spend much of his life trying to show people how great his ideas were. Many of them were 'years before their time'. People thought he was crazy when he promised a 'wireless broadcasting system'* to send pictures and sounds around the world. They laughed at him when he said he could send energy waves through water to detect* German submarines at the beginning of the First World War. Tesla had so many brilliant ideas, but he made very little money from them. And that money he used again on his next invention.

These days we can see Tesla's inventions all around us. We all use AC current in our homes to power our computers and televisions. Militaries* around the world use radar to defend* their countries. These and many others are all inventions from the brilliant mind of Nikola Tesla.

VOCABULARY
***invent** – erfinden; **hydroelectric power plant** – Wasserkraftwerk; **AC electrical current** – Wechselstrom; **DC electrical current** – Gleichstrom; **invested** – investiert (haben); **power up** – einschalten; **wireless broadcasting system** – ein drahtloses Sendesystem; **detect** – aufspüren; **military** – Militär; **defend** – verteidigen

SB p. 66

Castaway!

Chuck worked for a worldwide delivery company* in the USA. It was his job to get the really important parcels to their addresses. He often had to travel great distances with these parcels. He had to travel across land and sea so he could safely deliver them to the places written on them.

One night Chuck was travelling with a parcel on one of the company's planes when the plane got into a huge tropical storm. There was nothing the pilot could do as the plane fell from the night sky into the ocean below.

Chuck woke up. He was lying on a golden sandy beach. He had cuts all over his body. He was in a lot of pain. His clothes were wet and torn*. For a while he remembered nothing, but then his memories came back. He remembered the plane hitting the water. He remembered seeing the island at night in the light of the flashes of lightning* in the sky. He remembered swimming towards the island. He remembered how he was almost dying as he was climbing over the rocks.

The first few hours were full of hope. He hoped maybe the pilot was also somewhere on the island. He hoped they would soon find him. He was happy to be alive. There were a few parcels from the plane on the beach. Chuck didn't open them. He still hoped to deliver them unopened one day. But as the hours turned into days, the hope slowly disappeared. One day the dead body of the pilot washed up on the beach. Chuck buried* his friend in the sand. There was no rescue plane coming. Chuck was on his own.

Now he had to use all his energy to survive. He had to learn how to make a fire. It took him days. When he finally saw some flames, he laughed with joy. He couldn't just survive on coconut water. He had to le-arn how to catch fish. It took him days and when he finally caught one he cried with happiness. He built himself a shelter from the rain, he built himself a bed from coconut tree leaves. He didn't want to die on this island and he did everything he could to survive. One day he decided to open the parcels. There was little in them – just clothes and a volleyball with 'Wilson' written on it. Chuck looked at the ball. Using ash from the fire he drew a mouth and two eyes on it. Now Chuck had a friend. His name was 'Wilson'. There was still one parcel left. 'Anna Bracebridge, Jacksonville, USA' the address on it said. Chuck was not sure why, but he decided to leave it unopened.

As the years went by, Chuck got so used to the island that he knew it as well as he knew his hometown. And Chuck got used to 'having conversations' with Wilson. In his imagination, the volleyball wasn't a ball any more, he was a person. Chuck told him about his life back in the USA. He told him about his dreams for the future. He shared Chuck's hopes when occasionally a ship passed by far away on the horizon. He shared his sadness as the ship disappeared.

Then one day Chuck woke up and knew he could stay on the island no longer. He had to get back home even if it killed him. From now on he spent every day building a raft from pieces of wood he found on the island. He took his time. After a few months he was finally happy with his work. He picked up Wilson and put him on the raft. He put the unopened parcel next to him. Chuck pushed the raft into the water and jumped on.

VOCABULARY: *delivery company – Zustellfirma; **torn** – zerrissen; **flash of lightning** – Blitzstrahl; **bury** – begraben

Acknowledgements

The publishers would like to thank the following for their kind permission to reproduce the following photographs and other copyright material:

p28 Jaguar (Bethany), p42 Photo 12 (Rosa Parks), p60 Pictorial Press Ltd, p62 Pictorial Press Ltd **/ Alamy**; p19 Filippo Romeo (skiing in the Alps) / Paul Topp (surfing in Hawaii) / Josefkubes (climbing in Scotland), p22 Paul Topp, p26 Nadiia Gerbish (Oxford Street) / Pierre Jean Durieu (Hyde Park), p28 Pojoslaw (George, Alessia), p36 Georgesheldon, p44 Nickolay Stanev (Alcatraz) / F11photo (Golden Gate Bridge) / Joshua Rainey (China Town) / Kropic (cable car) / Rafael Ben Ari (aquarium), p45 Nancy Dressel, p48 Juliengrondin (volcano) / Roman Lysogor (avalanche), p49 Roger Rosentreter, p50 Dan Ross, p56 Per Björkdahl (plane), p65 Pojoslaw **I Dreamstime.com**; p14, p20, p21, p44 (San Francisco) / (Fisherman's Wharf), p48 (forest fire) / (tsunami), p56 (hippo) / (leopard), p57 **/ Pixabay**; **Wikimedia Commons** p16 cover image of King Kong, p28 Metilsteiner (James Holman, https://commons.wikimedia.org/wiki/File:HOLMAN(1840)_p008_JAMES_HOLMAN.jpg), p33 Paul Clarke (Creative Commons License 4.0 International, https://commons.wikimedia.org/wiki/File:Sir_Tim_Berners-Lee.jpg), p42 Dick DeMarsico (Martin Luther King Jr.), p66 p94 Adam Cuerden (Nikola Tesla, https://commons.wikimedia.org/wiki/File:N.Tesla.JPG); **Wikipedia** p16 Universal Pictures (Jaws) / Dreamworks Animation (Shrek); p16 cover images of The Lion King / The Emperor's New Groove **I Wikia**
Cover image by Charlotte Mcpherson
Commissioned Photography & Production by Studio Antonietti p28 (Oliver)

Every effort has been made to trace the owners of any copyright material in this book. If notified, the publishers will be pleased to rectify any errors or omissions.